FROM SIDE HUSTLE TO SUCCESS

TURNING YOUR PASSION INTO A THRIVING CAREER

JAY LAMBERT

2023 © SORADA PRESS
A COGITO MEDIA COMPANY

CONTENTS

- Common challenges and pitfalls in a side hustle
- Strategies for overcoming self-doubt and imposter syndrome
- Building confidence and resilience

- The importance of self-care in a side hustle
- Signs of stress and burnout
- Strategies for managing stress and keeping
  a healthy work-life balance

- The benefits of a side hustle for career development
- Identifying opportunities for growth and advancement
- Making the transition from a side hustle to a full-time career

- Assessing the potential for growth
- Developing a plan for scaling your side hustle
- Managing the challenges of growth and expansion

- The importance of diversifying your income as a side hustler
- Identifying additional income streams and opportunities
- Balancing multiple sources of income

- The role of personal branding in a side hustle
- Identifying your unique value proposition and messaging
- Building a strong personal brand online and offline

"Good things
happen to those
who hustle."

— *Anais Nin*

INTRODUCTION

Hey there! My name is Jay Lambert, and I'm the author of "From Side Hustle to Success: Turning Your Passion into a Thriving Career." I wrote this book because I know how hard it can be to turn your passion into a successful business. I've been there myself. I started my own business as a side hustle and, after a lot of perseverance, many long days, late nights and months of hard work, it finally took off. But it wasn't easy, and I had to learn a lot of things the hard way.

That's why I wanted to share my experience and the lessons I've learned with you. This book is all about how to take your passion and turn it into a thriving career. I'll show you how to identify your target market, create a business plan, and market your business effectively. I'll also share some inspiring personal stories from people I know, and all the tips to overcome struggles and find success I've learned along the way.

I wrote this book for anyone who has a passion they want to turn into a business. Whether you're just starting out or looking to take your existing side hustle to the next level, this book is for you. I hope it will be a valuable resource as you take the leap and turn your passion into a thriving career.

"The biggest adventure you can ever take is to live the life of your dreams."

– Oprah Winfrey

CHAPTER 1:
WHAT IS A SIDE HUSTLE AND WHY DO YOU NEED ONE?

Everyone has heard the saying "Don't give up your day job!" as a disparaging throwaway line to a friend who, maybe offered a witty line as a comedian might, or broke into a wobbly voice to sing a line from a hit song. We know the principle: stick to what you're good at, stay in your lane, keep the pennies rolling in.

But many of us do have passions for other things: a call-centre negotiator who dreams of making people laugh, or a pharmacist who would love to sing. Less performatively, maybe you're an accountant who yearns to write novels, or a social media manager who wants to sell vintage clothes. The point is this: everyone has a passion project, just like we all need a job to pay the bills.

So: enter the side hustle.

A side hustle could be any type of work that someone engages in outside of their full-time job to make extra income. This could include starting a small business, freelancing, or participating in the gig economy. Even doing performing music or comedy routines!

For these and many other people, a side hustle is a great way to turn their passions and interests into a source of income. It's a chance for individuals to explore new opportunities and try out different career paths, without making a full-time commitment. That thing you would love to do full-time, if only it paid enough? Well, here's how to get started…

When it comes to turning a side hustle into a successful career, it's important to remember that it will take hard work and dedication to make it happen. However, with the right mindset and approach, I believe that anyone can turn their passion into a thriving business.

There can be many benefits to starting a side hustle. One of the greatest is that it allows individuals to explore their interests and passions in a way that is often not possible through their full-time job. For example, if you're an artist who has always dreamed of turning your art into a business, a side hustle can be a great way to test the waters and see if there is a market for your work. An artist who keeps their main bills being paid by continuing in their day job can get a real sense over time of how their art develops, without the dispiriting sensation that the art (like most products) ultimately may have to equate to money.

Additionally, a side hustle can provide a source of financial stability, allowing individuals to save for the future or pay off debt. Even a few hundred dollars more every month might be the difference between a future home deposit, or earlier retirement, or help for your children's college fund.

Another benefit of having a side hustle is the sense of autonomy it can bring. It allows you to be your own boss, set your own schedule and priorities. It gives the flexibility to adjust your income to your life, rather than adjusting your life to your income. Most people who find their lives improved by their side hustle cite this independence, and the possibilities it offers for their future, as one of the main early wins.

Passion and purpose are key factors in a successful side hustle. When individuals can turn their passions into a source of income, they are more likely to be engaged and motivated in their work. Additionally, having a clear sense of purpose can help individuals stay focused on their goals and overcome any challenges that may arise. It's important to have a clear vision of what you want to achieve with your side hustle, and to stay focused on that vision even when things get tough.

Look, it's important to be aware that starting a side hustle isn't easy, and it will take a lot of hard work and dedication to make it successful. But with the right approach, I believe anyone can turn their passion into a growing business. By taking the time to clearly define your goals and purpose, and by staying focused and dedicated to your vision, you can turn your side hustle into a successful career.

With a side hustle, the opportunities are limitless, and the potential for success is great, if you are willing to put in the time and effort to make it happen.

Come on, let's get hustling!

TAKEAWAY TIPS:
1. A side hustle is a source of income that is pursued in addition to one's primary job, often as a means of generating extra income or pursuing a passion.
2. Starting a side hustle can provide multiple benefits, including increased financial stability, the opportunity to pursue one's passions and interests, and the ability to gain new skills and experiences.
3. Passion and purpose are key factors in the success of a side hustle. When you are passionate about what you're doing,

you're more likely to put in the extra effort and stay motivated to make it successful.

4. It's important to keep in mind that a side hustle is not a guarantee of success, but it's a great way to test the waters, validate an idea, and potentially grow it into a full-time business.

5. A side hustle can also help to build a safety net and provide an additional income stream to help you achieve your financial goals.

"Your work is going to fill a large part of your life, and the only way to be truly satisfied is to do what you believe is great work. And the only way to do great work is to love what you do. If you haven't found it yet, keep looking. Don't settle. As with all matters of the heart, you'll know when you find it."

— Steve Jobs

CHAPTER 2:
IDENTIFYING YOUR PASSION AND PURPOSE

Before starting a side hustle, you need to take the time to identify your passions and purpose. This will ensure that you are starting a business that you believe it, that aligns with your interests, values, and skills, and that has the potential to be successful.

Assessing your interests, values, and skills is a great place to start. Take some time to think about the things that you are truly passionate about, the causes that you believe in, and the skills and abilities that you have. Try to identify patterns and themes that emerge, as these can help point you in the direction of a potential side hustle.

This is a list of possible side-hustles, just to inspire you. But remember that the key is the side hustle needs to be something YOU love to do. There's no point in pursuing time and opportunities that you are not passionate about. Use this list as a starting point for your imagination!

1. Online tutoring or teaching
2. Pet-sitting or dog-walking
3. Home cleaning, streamlining or organization
4. Personal shopping or styling

5. Virtual assistant services

6. Social media management

7. Event planning or coordination

8. Graphic design or photography

9. Handyman or repair services

10. Personal training or fitness instruction

11. Car detailing or washing

12. Website design or development

13. Transcription or translation services

14. Beauty or hair services

15. Food delivery or weekly meal preparation

16. Online marketplaces like Etsy or Amazon Handmade

17. Ridesharing or delivery driver

18. Voiceover or podcast recording

19. Writing or content creation

20. Consulting or coaching services

21. Online survey taking

22. Stock trading or investment management

23. Freelance writing or editing

24. Virtual bookkeeping or accounting services

25. Selling products on online platforms like Amazon or eBay

26. Renting out a room on Airbnb

27. Dropshipping or e-commerce

28. Online course creation or tutoring

29. Affiliate marketing or influencer work

30. Voice acting or commercial work

31. Online language tutoring

32. Customized cake or pastry making

33. Home renovation or remodelling

34. Digital marketing or SEO services

35. Landscaping or gardening services

36. Customized t-shirt or clothing design

37. Personal styling or fashion consulting

38. Online personal shopping

39. Pet grooming or pet photography

40. Customized handmade jewellery or craft creation

41. Stand-up comedian

42. Musician or singer

Once you have a better understanding of your passions and skills, it's important to find your unique selling proposition (USP). This is the unique value that your side hustle will offer to customers. It could be a unique product or service, a particular approach you take to solving a problem, or even the way you market or position your business. Having a strong USP is what will set your side hustle apart from the competition and make it more attractive to potential customers.

With your USP in mind, it's time to develop a vision and mission statement for your side hustle.

Your vision statement should be a clear and concise statement of what you want to achieve with your business. It should be inspiring and motivating, and it should be something that you can refer to anytime when you need to stay focused on your goals. Keep it pinned to your desktop, somewhere you can see it every day.

Your mission statement, on the other hand, should be a detailed and practical statement of how you plan to achieve your vision. It should outline the steps that you will take to make your vision a reality. This is more of a working document that can evolve over time, keeping an eye on how you see the side hustle developing.

Having clear vision and mission statements will help keep you focused on your goals and ensure that you are making progress towards achieving them. They can also serve as a powerful motivator and guide if – and when – things get tough.

It's important to remember that finding your passion and purpose is an ongoing process. As you start your side hustle, you'll likely learn more about yourself and your passions, and your vision and mission most likely will evolve over time. But taking the time to identify your passions and purpose and developing a clear vision and mission for your side hustle, is an essential step in turning your side hustle into a successful career.

Assessing your interests, values, and skills, finding your unique selling proposition, and developing a vision and mission statement are all important steps in this process. By taking the time to understand what drives you and your target audience, you'll be better equipped to create a business that is both fulfilling and profitable.

TAKEAWAY TIPS:

1. Take the time to assess your interests, values, and skills to understand what you're truly passionate about and what you're good at. This will help you find a side hustle that aligns with your strengths and interests.

2. Finding your unique selling proposition (USP) is an important step in developing a successful side hustle. Your USP is what sets your offering apart from your competitors and will help you stand out in the market.

3. Developing a vision and mission statement for your side hustle will help you focus on your ultimate goal and the bigger picture of what you want to achieve.

4. Research and explore different options, don't limit yourself to one idea, explore different possibilities, don't be afraid of trying new things.

5. Connect your passions and skills with the current market trends to create a successful side hustle.

"I knew that if I failed
I wouldn't regret that,
but I knew the one thing
I might regret is not
trying."

– Jeff Bezos

CHAPTER 3:
FROM SIDE HUSTLE TO SUCCESS: DEFINING YOUR TARGET MARKET AND NICHE

As you embark on this exciting journey to turn your passion into a growing career, it's essential to first understand who your ideal customer is and where your side hustle fits in the market. This is the key to building a successful business and standing out among the competition.

When it comes to identifying your ideal customer, be as specific as possible. Consider factors such as age, gender, income, and location (collectively known as demographics), as well as their opinions, interests and pain points (known as psychographics). The more you understand about your target market, the better equipped you will be to create products or services that truly meet their needs.

Once you have a clear understanding of your ideal customer, it's time to take a good hard look at your competition. Find other businesses that offer similar products or services and see what they're doing well and what they're not. This information can help you to differentiate your offering and position your side hustle in a way that sets it apart from the rest.

Now that you have a clear profile of your target market and competition, it's time to define your niche. A niche is a specific area of the market that you want to focus on. This could be a specific type of product, a particular target market, or a unique location. The narrower your niche, the easier it will be to stand out from the competition. For example, instead of baking cakes as a side hustle, you might choose to focus only on the wedding cake market, as the deliveries would be weekend focused. You might assess that fits your personal weekly schedule better than the orders that could otherwise come in any time of the week when you need to focus on your day job.

As in the last chapter, in defining your niche, you should also position your side hustle in the market: this is the unique selling point of your products or services. This will be the value proposition, your promise that makes you different from competitors and solutions that you offer that is not available on the market, it will help you to define your brand and attract the right customers.

Keep in mind that as the market changes and evolves over time, so should your target market and niche. Regularly re-evaluating your strategy will ensure that your side hustle stays relevant and continues to grow.

Remember, starting a business is never easy, but with the right approach, it's possible to turn your passion into a prosperous career. By understanding your target market, identifying your competition and defining your niche, you'll be well on your way to building a successful business.

TAKEAWAY TIPS:

1. Understand your ideal customer by researching their demographics, psychographics, and behaviours. This will help you identify their needs and pain points and target your marketing efforts effectively.

2. Identify your competition and analyse their strengths and weaknesses to differentiate your offering and stand out in the market.

3. Defining your niche and positioning your side hustle in the market is crucial to reach the right audience and establish your business as an authority in your field.

4. Use customer feedback to improve and evolve your product or service to better meet their needs.

5. Continuously analyse your target market and niche to stay up-to-date with changes and adapt your side hustle accordingly.

EXAMPLE:

For Maria, who wanted to grow a fashion design business, identifying her target market was a significant challenge. She didn't know who her ideal customer was or how to differentiate her offering from her competitors. She felt like her business lacked direction and focus.

To overcome this challenge, Maria decided to conduct market research and analyse her competition. She reached out to her initial customers to gather feedback and understand their needs and preferences. This was a highly instructive process and immediately she learned some aspects of her business she could improve on.

Maria researched her competition in detail, both online and with some test purchases, and she identified their target markets and offerings. From there, she was far better able to define her own target market and develop a unique value proposition that differentiated her from her competitors. She began to focus on a specific niche within the fashion industry and started to position her business accordingly.

Through these targeted efforts, Maria was able to sharply define her target market and niche, which helped her to focus her efforts and resources. She learned that understanding her ideal customer is crucial for developing a successful business strategy, and that researching the competition and differentiating her offering is key to standing out in the market. She also realized that focusing on a specific niche could help to position her business as an expert in that field. She started to see an increase in sales and customer satisfaction as a rapid result of her efforts.

"The best time to plant a tree was 20 years ago. The second best time is now."

— Chinese Proverb

CHAPTER 4:
CREATING A BUSINESS PLAN AND SETTING GOALS

I cannot stress this enough: when it comes to turning your side hustle into a successful career, one of the most important steps you can take is to create a business plan. A business plan is a document that outlines your business concept, target market, financial projections, and strategy for achieving your goals. It's the roadmap that will help guide you as you build and grow your business. It sounds complicated but it really needn't be.

A well-written business plan can help you:
- Clearly define your business concept and objectives
- Identify and target the right market for your products or services
- Estimate the costs and potential revenue of your business
- Secure funding from investors or lenders
- Monitor your progress and set adjustments as needed

The Elements of a Successful Business Plan:
- Executive Summary: A brief overview of your business concept, target market, and financial projections.

- Business Description: A more detailed explanation of your business, including the products or services you offer, the problem you're solving, and your unique selling points.
- Market Analysis: An analysis of the market you're entering, including information on your target customer, your competition, and the industry trends.
- Sales and Marketing Strategy: An explanation of how you plan to promote your products or services and generate sales.
- Financial Projections: A detailed forecast of your income and expenses, including projections for your start-up costs, revenue, and profitability.

When creating your business plan, it's important to be as specific and realistic as possible. Use data and research to support your assumptions and projections, and be sure to review and update your plan regularly as your business grows and evolves. You may choose to share this with a friend to help you define your goals, or you might find it useful later with a financing option such as a bank manager or investor.

In addition to creating a business plan, it's also important to set specific goals for your side hustle. Goals can help you stay focused and motivated, and will provide a clear sense of direction for your business. However, it's important to set goals that are specific, measurable, attainable, relevant, and time-bound, known as SMART goals.

SMART Goals:

- Specific: Goals should be clear and specific, with a defined outcome.
- Measurable: Goals should be quantifiable so you can track your progress.

- <u>Attainable</u>: Goals should be realistic and achievable.
- <u>Relevant</u>: Goals should align with your overall business objectives.
- <u>Time-bound</u>: Goals should have a deadline for completion.

So, examples of SMART goals for a side hustle could be:

- Increase sales by 15% within the next 6 months.
- Increase website traffic by 30% within the next year.
- Launch a new product or service within the next 12 months.

By creating a business plan and setting SMART goals, you'll be well on your way to turning your side hustle into a robust career. Remember, creating a business plan is an ongoing process, not a one-time task. You should always be evaluating, adjusting and updating it as you move forward, and setting new goals as you reach the old ones.

TAKEAWAY TIPS:

1. A business plan is an essential tool for any side hustle. It should include elements such as an overview of your business, a market analysis, financial projections, and a marketing strategy.

2. A successful business plan should be clear, concise, and realistic, and should also be reviewed and updated regularly.

3. Setting SMART (Specific, Measurable, Achievable, Relevant, Time-bound) goals for your side hustle can help you stay on track and measure your progress.

4. Regularly review your business plan and goals, and adjust them as needed to stay on track to achieve your objectives.

5. Use your business plan as a guide to stay focused and on track, it will help you make important business decisions, and identify opportunities for growth.

CHAPTER 5:
BUILDING YOUR ONLINE PRESENCE

In today's digital age, building an online presence has long been crucial for any business, and that includes a side hustle. A website, an email list, and an active social media presence will help you reach a wider audience, generate leads, and grow your business.

A website can serve as an online storefront for your products or services and give you a professional presence online. It also gives potential customers a place to go to learn more about your business and what you have to offer.

A website can be used in many ways:

- Presenting your products or services
- Providing information about your business
- Generating leads through contact forms or opt-ins
- Showcasing customer testimonials and reviews
- Sharing blog posts or articles to educate and engage with your audience
- Creating a sense of trust and credibility with your target market

In addition to having a website, it's also important to build an email list and a following on social media. An email list allows you to directly reach out to potential customers, while a social media following can help you expand your reach and create a sense of community around your business.

Building an email list can be done by offering a lead magnet such as an e-book, webinar, or a checklist in exchange for an email address. There are many ways to go about this that are creative and interesting, and they will lead to a solid list of people who have opted-in to the idea of your business. Once you have people on your email list, you can send them regular updates about your business, new products or services, and special promotions.

Social media platforms like Facebook, Instagram, Twitter, and LinkedIn can be leveraged to connect with your target market. Social media provides a platform for you to share your expertise, engage with your audience, and build brand awareness. It's also a great way to drive traffic to your website and generate leads.

Creating valuable and relevant content is a key aspect of building your online presence. This could include blog posts, videos, infographics, and more. Again, it is a creative process that the internet can give you many ideas for. Use your imagination! By providing value to your social audience, you'll attract new visitors to your website and social media channels, and this enables you to encourage them to take action.

Engaging with your audience is also critical. Responding to comments, answering questions, and providing support can help build trust and loyalty among your customers. Actively engaging with your followers will also help you understand their pain points and preferences, which can inform your marketing and product development strategy. Pain points are critical for you to understand for your business: it may be a price ceiling over which the product drops off in demand, or the speed of delivery which is crucial, or almost anything that defines the difference between a sale – or a fail.

Creating a solid online presence inevitably takes time and effort, but it's worth it in the long run. By building a website, email list, and social media following, and consistently creating valuable content and engaging with your audience, you'll be able to attract new customers and grow your business.

TAKEAWAY TIPS:

1. A website is an essential tool for any side hustle, it's a great way to establish your brand, showcase your products or services, and reach a wider audience.

2. Building an email list and social media following is an important step in building your online presence. This will allow you to communicate with your audience, promote your offerings, and grow your customer base.

3. Creating high-quality content and engaging with your audience online will help you establish yourself as an authority in your field, build trust with your customers, and increase your visibility.

EXAMPLE:

James, who runs a photography business, found building an online presence a significant challenge. He didn't have a website, and as a middle-aged man, he realised he didn't know how to best use social media or email marketing to reach potential customers. He felt like he was missing out on valuable opportunities to promote his business online.

To overcome this, James decided to invest in building a website and learning about digital marketing. He hired a web designer to create a website for his business that showcased his portfolio and services. He also started to learn about social media marketing and began to build a following on Instagram and Facebook. Additionally, he started to build an email list by offering a free e-book in exchange for signing up to his mailing list.

Through his efforts, James was able to build a strong online presence for his business. He learned that having a professional website was crucial for showcasing his services and portfolio, and that social media and email marketing can be powerful tools to reach potential customers. He also realized that creating engaging content and building a relationship with his audience would be essential for growing his business. He started to see an increase in inquiries and bookings as a result of all his online efforts. Within six months the investment in an online strategy had been recouped.

CHAPTER 6:
NETWORKING AND BUILDING PARTNERSHIPS

Networking and building partnerships are important aspects of any business, and for a side hustle it is no exception. Networking allows you to connect with other professionals and entrepreneurs, learn from their experiences, and gain exposure for your business. Building partnerships could help you expand your reach, gain new customers, and achieve your business goals.

Networking is essential for a side hustle, as it can help you:

- Expand your reach and gain exposure for your business
- Learn from other professionals and entrepreneurs
- Create opportunities for collaborations
- Access new customers, suppliers, partners, or investors
- Stay informed about industry trends and developments
- Gain valuable insights and feedback on your business
- Establish a sense of community and support around your business

Building meaningful relationships and partnerships requires effort and dedication. Here are some strategies you can use to build strong connections and partnerships:

- Attend networking events and conferences: These events provide a great opportunity to meet new people, make connections, and learn about new trends and developments in your industry.
- Participation within online communities: Online communities such as LinkedIn groups or Facebook groups provide a great platform for connecting with like-minded professionals and entrepreneurs.
- Leverage social media: Social media platforms can be used to build connections and partnerships. Follow and engage with other professionals and entrepreneurs in your industry, and consider using tools like LinkedIn's "Introduce" feature to connect with people in your network who may be able to help you achieve your business goals.
- Offer value: Building relationships and partnerships is not just about what you can gain; it's also about what you can offer. Consider ways you can help others, whether through mentoring, collaborations, or providing valuable resources.
- Follow up and stay in touch: Building relationships and partnerships is not a one-time event. It requires continuous effort to maintain and strengthen the connection. Follow up with people you've met, schedule check-ins, and make an effort to stay in touch.

Once you have built a strong network of connections and partnerships, you can leverage these relationships to help grow your side hustle. Here are some ways you can leverage your network to achieve your business goals:

- Ask for referrals: Ask your network to refer your products or services to their own networks.

- Collaborate on projects or initiatives: Partner with other businesses or entrepreneurs to achieve mutual goals.
- Seek advice and feedback: Ask your network for advice and feedback on your business, products or services.
- Promote each other: Use your network to promote each other's businesses and services.

Networking and building partnerships are essential for any business, and a side hustle is no exception. By putting in the effort to build meaningful relationships and partnerships, you can expand your reach, gain new customers, and achieve your business goals.

TAKEAWAY TIPS:

1. Networking is an important aspect of any side hustle, it helps to build meaningful relationships, expose you to new opportunities, and expand your reach.
2. Building partnerships can help you tap into new markets, gain access to new resources, and leverage the strengths of others to grow your side hustle.
3. Leveraging your network to grow your side hustle can help you achieve your goals faster and with more resources.

CHAPTER 7:
PRICING YOUR SERVICES AND PRODUCTS

Pricing your services and products is a critical aspect of any business, including a side hustle. Getting the pricing right can mean the difference between success and failure. Setting the right price can help you attract customers, generate profit, and ensure the sustainability of your business.

The first step in pricing your services or products is to understand the value that they offer to your customers. This means considering the costs of production, the target market, the competition, and the unique value proposition that sets your offering apart.

To determine the value of your offering, you should:

- Understand your target market: Research your target market to understand their needs, wants, and buying habits.
- Understand your costs: Consider the costs of production, including materials, labour, and overhead costs.
- Understand your competition: Research your competition to understand their pricing strategies and the value they offer to customers.

- Understand your unique value proposition: Identify the unique value that your products or services offer to customers.

Once you understand the value of your offering, you can determine your pricing strategy. There are different pricing strategies you can choose from, depending on your business goals, target market and industry.

Here are some common pricing strategies:

- Cost-plus pricing: Pricing based on the costs of production, plus a markup to generate profit.
- Value-based pricing: Pricing based on the value that your products or services offer to customers.
- Competitive pricing: Pricing based on the prices of your competitors.
- Dynamic pricing: Adjusting prices based on market demand and conditions.

In addition to determining your prices, it's also important to be able to negotiate with both clients and partners. Negotiating effectively can help you to close deals, secure better terms and build long-lasting relationships.

There are many books specific to the – considerable! – skill of negotiating, but here are some simple tips for negotiating when starting out your side hustle:

- Understand the other party's perspective: Understand the other party's needs, wants and priorities, it will make it easier to reach a mutually beneficial agreement.
- Communicate your value proposition: Clearly communicate the value that your products or services offer to the other party, and how they will benefit from working with you. This can much less obvious than you think at first, it may be that

price is less of a sticking point than the ability to agree to do the work at the drop of a hat. Think about what it involves for you to modify your offering.

- Be prepared to compromise. Negotiations most often involve compromise, be prepared to make concessions if necessary to get an agreement over the line.
- Conversely, be willing to walk away: Know what your bottom line is and be prepared to walk away if the deal does not meet your needs.

Pricing your services and products is a critical aspect of any business. Determining the value of your offering, determining the pricing strategy, and negotiating effectively with clients and partners can help you attract customers, generate profit, and ensure the sustainability of your business.

TAKEAWAY TIPS:

1. Understanding the value of your offering is critical to pricing your services or products effectively. It's important to consider factors such as your costs, competition, and target market when determining your prices.

2. Developing a pricing strategy that aligns with your goals and target market will help you to position your side hustle in the market and attract the right customers.

3. Negotiating with clients and partners is an important aspect of pricing your services or products. It's important to be flexible and willing to compromise to close deals and build long-term relationships.

EXAMPLE:

For Alex, who set up a consulting side hustle, pricing his services was a significant challenge. At first, he didn't know how to determine the right prices for his services and struggled to negotiate with clients and partners. He often under-priced his services and for some time didn't feel confident in his pricing decisions.

To overcome this challenge, Alex decided to research and study different pricing strategies and models. He learned about value-based pricing, cost-plus pricing, and competitive pricing. He also learned about how to determine the value of his services and how to communicate that value to potential clients. He also began to work on building his negotiation skills, by learning about different techniques and strategies for negotiating effectively.

Through his efforts, Alex was able to determine a pricing strategy that was fair and profitable for his business. He learned that understanding the value of his services and communicating that value to potential clients was key to determining the right prices. He also realized that having effective negotiation skills is crucial for closing deals and building long-term relationships with clients and partners. Within a quarter he started to see an increase in revenue and more satisfied clients.

CHAPTER 8:
MARKETING AND SALES STRATEGIES

Marketing and sales are essential for any business, and a side hustle is no exception. They are the driving force behind any business that aims to attract new customers, generate revenue, and grow.

Effective marketing and sales strategies will help you:

- Reach and attract new customers
- Build brand awareness and credibility
- Generate leads and sales
- Scale and grow your business

Without a solid marketing and sales strategy, your side hustle may struggle to find new customers and revenue, which can make it difficult to sustain and grow the business.

To effectively market and sell your products or services, you need to identify the channels and tactics that will be most effective for reaching your target market. This could include:

- Social media marketing
- Content marketing
- Influencer marketing
- Email marketing
- Referral marketing
- Paid advertising

- Public relations
- Word of mouth

Rank these options for your side hustle, even if you think it might be too early to use, for example, paid advertising. It is important to evaluate the strengths and weaknesses of each channel and tactic, and to prioritise the ones that are most likely to reach and engage your target market.

In addition to marketing, you also need to develop a sales process that will help you convert leads into customers. A sales process will typically include several stages, including:

- Prospecting: Identifying and qualifying potential customers
- Presenting: Giving a presentation or demonstration of your products or services
- Handling objections: Addressing any concerns or objections that may arise
- Closing: Closing the deal by securing an agreement or commitment
- Following up: Following up with the customer after the sale

Building a sales process that is tailored to your specific business can help you convert more leads into paying customers. You will only know with experience what this process entails, and will you need to know it inside-out so that you can streamline it for efficiency.

To achieve a sustainable and growing business, it is vital to have a marketing and sales strategy in place, identifying and using the right channels and tactics that will reach and engage your target market. Put time into developing a well-structured sales process that takes prospects through the process of becoming customers and retain them, helping to close deals and boost revenue.

TAKEAWAY TIPS:

1. Marketing and sales are essential for any side hustle, it's important to identify your target market, understand their needs and wants, and create a marketing and sales strategy that effectively reaches them.

2. Identifying the right marketing channels and tactics for your side hustle is crucial, it will help you reach your target audience more effectively and increase your conversions.

3. Building a sales process and closing deals is an important step in growing your side hustle, it's important to understand your customer's needs, build trust, and close the deal.

EXAMPLE:

Running a small online store that sells eco-friendly products, Travis found that marketing and sales were a challenge. He had a small customer base and struggled to reach new potential customers and generate sales. He didn't know how to market his products and had no sales process in place.

To overcome this challenge, Travis decided to take a course on digital marketing and sales. He learned about various marketing channels, such as SEO (search engine optimisation), PPC (pay-per-click online advertising), social media, and email marketing, as well as how to use them effectively. He also learned about how to build a sales process, from lead generation to closing deals. He started to implement these strategies and started to see results.

Through his efforts, Travis was able to increase his customer base and generate more sales. He learned that a well-executed marketing strategy is essential for reaching new customers and driving sales. He also realized that having a clear sales process in place is crucial for closing deals and growing his business. He rapidly started to see a significant increase in his revenue and was able to expand his product line.

"You miss 100% of the shots you don't take."

– Wayne Gretzky

CHAPTER 9:
TIME MANAGEMENT AND PRODUCTIVITY

Managing time and being productive are key factors in turning your side hustle into a successful career. Balancing your side hustle with other responsibilities, such as work, family, and personal life, can be challenging. Setting boundaries and protecting your time can help you stay focused and make the most of your limited time.

A side hustle can be an exciting and fulfilling pursuit, but it's important to remember that it's only one aspect of your life. With proper planning, setting boundaries, and learning how to manage your time effectively, you can achieve a healthy work-life balance.

Here are some tips for balancing your side hustle with other responsibilities:

- Set clear priorities: Understand what is most important to you and what is not.
- Create a schedule: Create a schedule that allows you to devote time to your side hustle while still fulfilling your other responsibilities.
- Develop the confidence to say "no": Be selective about the opportunities you pursue and be willing to turn down things that do not align with your goals.

- Ask for help: Don't be afraid to ask for help from family and friends, especially for tasks like childcare or running errands. You may be able to help them back if they embark on a side hustle journey one day!
- Set aside time for self-care: Make sure to set aside time for yourself, to relax, recharge and take care of your physical and mental well-being.

Setting boundaries and protecting your time is crucial to your success. It can be easy to get caught up in your side hustle and neglect other areas of your life. Setting boundaries can help you stay focused on your goals and make the most of your limited time.

Here are some tips for setting boundaries and protecting your time:

- Set specific working hours: Determine when you will work on your side hustle and stick to those hours.
- Say "no" to non-essential tasks or distractions.
- Turn off notifications: Try to minimize distractions by turning off notifications on your phone or computer during your designated working hours.
- Set aside time for other activities: Make sure to set aside time for other activities such as exercise, spending time with family, and self-care.
- Limit multitasking: Multitasking can be detrimental to productivity, so try to focus on one task at a time.

To turn your side hustle into a burgeoning career, it is important to maximize your productivity and efficiency. Here are some strategies that can help:

- Prioritise your tasks: Prioritise tasks based on importance and urgency, and tackle the most important tasks first. This seems obvious but so many people put the jobs they don't like the look of down their to-do list, no matter how necessary or urgent they are. Learn to be ruthless with this activity.

- Use time management tools: Use tools like calendars, to-do lists, or time tracking apps to help you manage your time more effectively.
- Eliminate distractions: Eliminate distractions such as social media or unnecessary emails, to stay focused on the task at hand.
- Take breaks: Taking short breaks throughout the day can help you stay energized and refocused.
- Automate repetitive tasks: Automating repetitive tasks can help you save time and energy, so you can focus on more important tasks.

Managing your time and maximising how productive you are will be key factors in the success of turning your side hustle into a flourishing career. Balancing your side hustle with other responsibilities, setting boundaries and protecting your time, and using effective strategies for increasing productivity and efficiency can help you stay focused and make the most of your limited time.

TAKEAWAY TIPS:

1. Balancing your side hustle with other responsibilities can be challenging, so set boundaries and protect your time. Avoid burnout and maintain a healthy work-life balance.

2. Setting clear goals and prioritising tasks will help you stay focused and increase your productivity and efficiency.

3. Strategies for increasing productivity and efficiency include delegating tasks, using productivity tools, and eliminating distractions. Find what works best for you and stick to it.

CHAPTER 10:
FINANCIAL MANAGEMENT AND PLANNING

While it might take you away – for a few hours – from the thing you love to do, financial management and planning are critical for the success of any business, and that includes the side hustle. Understanding your financial needs and goals, setting up a budget, and tracking expenses can help you stay financially stable and achieve your business objectives.

The first step is to understand your financial needs and goals. This includes understanding your business's costs, revenue projections, and cash flow needs. It is also important to identify your personal financial goals, whether saving for retirement or paying off debt.

Set up a budget and track your expenses. A budget can help you prioritise expenses, plan for contingencies, and it will identify areas where you can cut costs.

When setting up a budget, be sure to include all expected income and expenses for your business, including fixed costs (such as rent and utilities) and variable costs (such as advertising and inventory). Be realistic and flexible with your budget and re-evaluate it periodically to ensure it aligns with your current financial situation.

It's also important to track your expenses. Keeping track of expenses can help you understand where your money is going and identify any unnecessary expenses. This can be done by keeping receipts, invoices, and bank statements, or by using accounting or expense tracking software. So many people fall into the trap of thinking that a side hustle is less than a real business, and shove receipts into a box. Don't be that person, make it matter of pride to set up simple reconciliations in spreadsheets and ensure paperwork is marked and filed. For a simple side hustle this should be an easy system to maintain.

As a side hustler, it's a fact of life that you may need financial support in order to grow and thrive. This could include seeking investment, loans or grants. It will also be helpful to seek advice from a financial advisor or accountant to help you with budgeting, tax planning, and other financial management tasks. The importance of good record-keeping for these purposes cannot be over-stated. It will save you valuable time – your time! – and allow external professionals to help you as quickly, efficiently, and therefore cheaply, as possible.

A good financial advisor or accountant will provide valuable insights and advice on budgeting, cash flow management, and forecasting, and can help you understand the financial aspects of your side hustle business. They can also help you understand financial terminology and concepts, and help you make informed decisions about your business finances. These relationships are going to be key to your success growing your side hustle. Don't neglect them.

It's important to stay informed about financial opportunities and resources that may be available to you, such as government grants or small business loans. It is also essential to be aware of relevant laws and regulations, and to make sure you are fully compliant with all tax and accounting requirements.

Financial management and planning are critical for the success of any business, including a side hustle. Understanding your financial needs and goals, setting up a budget, and tracking expenses are essential for staying financially stable and achieving your business objectives. Seeking financial support and advice from financial experts can help you better understand financial concepts and make informed decisions about your business finances.

TAKEAWAY TIPS:

1. Understanding your financial needs and goals is crucial to being able to budget and plan effectively. This includes understanding your income and expenses, as well as your short-term and long-term financial goals.

2. Setting up a budget and tracking expenses is an essential step in managing your finances. This will help you stay on top of your spending and ensure that you are using your money in the most effective way possible.

3. Seeking financial support and advice is an important part of building a successful side hustle. This can include seeking out financial advisors, finding funding sources, or working with a bookkeeper to manage your finances.

CHAPTER 11:
LEGAL AND REGULATORY CONSIDERATIONS

As your side hustle turns into a growing business, it's going to be increasingly important to understand your legal and regulatory obligations. Failure to comply with the laws and regulations that apply to your business might lead to serious legal and financial consequences, so it's crucial to be aware of your responsibilities from the outset.

One of the first things you'll need to consider is whether your business requires any licenses or permits to operate. These can vary depending on the type of business you're running, as well as the location in which you're operating. For example, if you're running any kind of food business, you'll most likely need to comply with national and local food safety regulations and to obtain any necessary licenses. If you're providing a service, such as counselling or consulting, you may need to be licensed by the state or country in which you're operating. It's important to research the specific requirements that apply to your business, and to obtain any necessary licenses or permits before you begin operating.

Another important consideration when starting any business is protecting your intellectual property. This includes branding, unique ideas, inventions, or original works that you've created as part of your business. For example, if you've developed a new product or process, you'll want to consider filing for a patent or trademark to protect it. Additionally, you'll need to be mindful of copyright laws when using any works that you didn't create yourself, such as music or photographs.

When you're starting a business, you'll also need to be familiar with contracts and legal documents. This can include agreements with suppliers, customers, and partners, as well as any necessary legal paperwork such as incorporation documents or employment agreements. It's important to understand the terms of these agreements and to seek legal advice if you have any questions or concerns.

In addition, you should also be aware of the laws related to employment and labour. This includes proper record keeping, compliance with minimum wage and overtime laws, and anti-discrimination laws. You should also be familiar with laws related to taxes, such as the requirement to register for a sales tax permit and collect and remit sales taxes, if applicable.

It's important to remember that as your business grows, you will be taking on more responsibilities and you should be aware of the legal and regulatory environment in which you are operating. It is always good practice to seek legal and accounting advice early on to ensure that your business is compliant with all the relevant regulations.

Remember that while legal compliance can be a daunting task, it is ultimately important to ensure that your business is operating within the law, and that it is protected from any legal liabilities. By taking the time to understand your legal and regulatory obligations, you can help to ensure the success and longevity of your business.

TAKEAWAY TIPS:

1. Understanding your legal and regulatory obligations as a side hustle is crucial to protect your business and avoid any legal issues down the road. This includes understanding local, state, and federal laws and regulations that may apply to your business.

2. Protecting your intellectual property could be a key consideration when building a side hustle. This includes looking into trademarking your business name and logo, registering any patents or copyrights you might have, and taking steps to protect any proprietary information or trade secrets.

3. Working with contracts and legal documents is an essential part of any business. It's important to understand the legal terms and conditions of any agreements you make and to have legal documents, such as contracts, in place to protect your interests.

EXAMPLE:

Laura, who runs a small baking business, found understanding and complying with food regulations was challenging. She was not familiar with all of the laws and regulations surrounding food production and sales, and found it difficult to navigate the complex rules and requirements.

To overcome this challenge, Laura first decided to take a food safety course, and then hired a food safety consultant to help her understand the regulations and requirements for her business. She began to research and stay up-to-date on the various laws and regulations related to her industry, including labelling, packaging, and sanitation requirements. Additionally, she started to document all her food safety procedures and keep detailed records to ensure compliance with the regulations.

Through her efforts, Laura was able to understand and comply with all the food regulations required for her business. She learned that staying informed and educated about the laws and regulations specific to her industry was crucial for running a legal and compliant business. She also realized that keeping detailed records and documentation is an important part of maintaining compliance with regulations, which helped her to protect her business and her customers.

CHAPTER 12:
BUILDING A TEAM AND DELEGATING TASKS

As your side hustle grows, you may find that you need to bring on additional help to manage the workload. Building a team could bring benefits to your business, including increased efficiency and productivity, as well as new perspectives and ideas. It can also help to alleviate some of the stress and pressure of running a business on your own.

The first step in building a team is identifying your team needs. This means taking a close look at the tasks and responsibilities that you're currently handling, and determining which ones could be delegated to others. For example, you may want to bring on a virtual assistant to handle administrative tasks, or a social media specialist to manage your online presence. By identifying your team needs, you'll be able to better focus on the tasks that are most critical to your business, and that you're best suited to handle.

When you're looking for team members, it's important to find the right fit. This means looking for people who share your vision and values, and who are excited about the work you're doing. It's also important to find people who have the skills and experience that you need. For example, if you're looking to bring on a marketing specialist, you'll want someone who has a strong background of marketing in your specific niche and has experience with the types of sales tactics that you're planning on using.

As you build your team, it's important to create a successful team dynamic. This means fostering open communication and collaboration, and setting clear expectations and goals. It also means creating a positive and supportive working environment, where team members feel valued and appreciated.

Delegating tasks is an important part of building a successful team. It means entrusting certain responsibilities to other team members and trusting them to handle it efficiently. This can be difficult at first, especially if you're used to handling everything yourself. However, by delegating tasks, you'll be able to free up your time and focus on the things that you do best. To delegate tasks effectively, it is important to be clear about your expectations and provide the necessary resources, tools, and training to your team members to help them succeed.

Another important aspect of delegation is setting up clear lines of communication and management oversight. This means setting up regular check-ins and progress reports, and being available to answer questions and provide guidance. It may also be important to establish clear performance metrics, to track the progress and performance of the delegated tasks and make necessary adjustments.

Building a team and delegating tasks is essential to growing your side hustle into a successful business. It can bring new ideas, skill sets and energy to the table and help you scale your business to the next level. By identifying your team needs, finding the right fit and creating a successful team dynamic, you can build a team that is committed to helping you achieve your goals.

TAKEAWAY TIPS:

1. The benefits of building a team for a side hustle include the ability to share the workload, gain new perspectives, and access new skills and expertise.

2. Identifying your team needs and finding the right fit is essential to building a successful team. This includes understanding the roles and responsibilities of each team member, as well as finding people who share your vision and values.

3. Delegating tasks and building a successful team dynamic is crucial for the growth of your side hustle. This includes setting clear expectations, providing feedback and support, and building trust and open communication within your team.

"Your most unhappy customers are your greatest source of learning."

– *Bill Gates*

CHAPTER 13:
CUSTOMER SERVICE AND RETENTION

One of the key elements of a successful side hustle is delivering excellent customer service. Customers who are satisfied with the service they receive are more likely to return, recommend your business to others, and provide positive feedback. In fact, studies have shown that customers who have a positive experience with a company are more likely to remain loyal and less likely to switch to a competitor.

Building customer loyalty and retention starts with creating a positive customer experience. This mean being responsive to customer needs, addressing any issues or concerns promptly, and providing high-quality products or services. It also means going above and beyond to meet customers' expectations and providing additional value. For example, you might offer a complimentary consultation or a free follow-up service.

One effective strategy for building customer loyalty is to create a sense of community around your brand. This can be done by hosting events, participating in local events or charities and fostering communication between customers through social media, email or other channels. By creating a sense of belonging and engagement, customers will feel more connected to your brand, which in turn will lead to increased loyalty and retention.

Another important aspect of providing excellent customer service is handling complaints and negative feedback. No business is perfect and there will be times when customers are not completely satisfied with the service they received. When this happens, and realistically it is a "when" and not an "if", it is important to handle the situation professionally and empathetically. This means acknowledging the complaint, taking ownership of the problem, and finding a resolution in a timely manner. It's also important to ensure that complaints and feedback are tracked, so that you can identify trends and take steps to prevent similar issues from arising in the future.

It is also crucial to show your customers that you value their feedback by taking action. Follow up with them to let them know what steps you have taken to improve your service and prevent similar issues from happening in the future. Showing that you are committed to continuous improvement and that you take their feedback seriously will help to build trust and strengthen your relationships with your customers.

In conclusion, providing excellent customer service is essential to building a successful side hustle. By focusing on creating a positive customer experience, building loyalty and retention and handling complaints and feedback effectively, you can create a strong foundation for your business and foster long-term relationships with your customers.

TAKEAWAY TIPS:

1. The importance of excellent customer service in a side hustle cannot be overstated. This includes providing a high level of customer service, being responsive to customer needs and feedback, and going above and beyond to meet customer expectations.

2. Strategies for building customer loyalty and retention include creating a positive customer experience, providing exceptional customer service, and offering rewards and incentives to repeat customers.

3. Handling complaints and negative feedback is an important part of customer service. This includes listening to customer complaints, addressing the issue in a timely manner, and taking steps to prevent similar issues in the future.

EXAMPLE:

For Tay, a small business owner who sold handmade candles, customer service was a sticking point. She had a small, loyal customer base, but she found it difficult to maintain customer loyalty and retention. She also struggled with handling complaints and negative feedback effectively.

To overcome this challenge, Tay decided to implement a few strategies. She began to actively engage with her customers, by sending personalized thank-you notes and following up with them after their purchase. She also started to ask for feedback and reviews from her customers, and used this feedback to improve her products and services. Additionally, she began to offer loyalty rewards and discounts to her repeat customers as a way to encourage repeat business.

Through her efforts, Tay was able to improve her customer service and retention. She learned that by engaging with her customers and actively seeking their feedback is crucial for building customer loyalty and retention. It was an unexpected intervention that headed off more serious complaints. Tay also came to understand that handling complaints and negative feedback effectively is an important part of providing excellent customer service. She began to see a significant increase in repeat customers and customer satisfaction, which helped her to grow her business.

CHAPTER 14:
STAYING MOTIVATED AND FOCUSED

Starting and growing a side hustle can be an exciting and rewarding experience, but it can also be challenging at times. It's important to remember that building a successful business takes time and effort, and it's natural to encounter setbacks and challenges along the way. Staying motivated and focused is crucial to overcoming these obstacles and achieving your goals.

One of the most effective ways to maintain motivation and focus is to remind yourself of why you started your side hustle in the first place. By staying true to your passion and purpose, you'll be more likely to stay motivated and invested in your business, even when things get tough. Revisit your vision statement and mission statement regularly to remind yourself. Additionally, it's important to set clear and achievable goals for yourself, and to track your progress towards achieving them. Having a clear sense of what you want to achieve will help you stay focused and motivated, and it will also give you a sense of satisfaction as you reach each milestone.

Another aspect of staying motivated and focused is to build a support system around you. This might include friends, family, business associates, or even finding a mentor. They can help you stay on track when things get tough, by providing guidance and advice, as well as a sounding board for your ideas. Additionally, it can also be helpful to join a community of like-minded individuals, such as a networking group or an online forum, where you can share your experiences and learn from others.

It's also important to be realistic about the challenges that come with starting a side hustle. There will be times when things don't go as planned and setbacks occur, but it's important to not get discouraged and to not take it personally. Instead, use these moments as opportunities for learning and growth. Reflect on what went wrong and use that insight to make changes and improve your business.

Additionally, taking care of yourself is important to maintain your motivation and focus. Make sure to schedule regular breaks, and set aside time for activities that you enjoy, whether it's going for a walk, reading a book, or spending time with friends and family. Self-care can help you to relax and recharge, which can be essential for maintaining motivation and focus over the long term. Sometimes a little time away from your side hustle can renew the vigour with which you started it.

Staying motivated and focused are going to be essential in turning your side hustle into a successful business. By staying true to your passion and purpose, setting clear goals, building a support system, and by taking care of yourself, you can overcome obstacles and setbacks and stay on track to achieving your goals.

TAKEAWAY TIPS:

1. Maintaining motivation and focus with a side hustle is crucial for achieving success. This includes setting clear goals, staying organized and on task, and taking time to reflect on your progress and celebrate your successes.

2. Coping with setbacks and challenges is a natural part of building a side hustle. It's important to stay positive and persistent, and to look for opportunities to learn and grow from difficult experiences.

3. Staying true to your passion and purpose is essential to staying motivated and focused. This includes staying focused on your goals, remaining dedicated to your vision, and staying true to your values and beliefs.

CHAPTER 15:
PERSONAL AND PROFESSIONAL DEVELOPMENT: THE JOURNEY OF LIFELONG LEARNING

As you strive to take your side hustle to the next level and turn it into a growing career, it's important to remember that personal and professional development is an ongoing process. It's a journey of lifelong learning, where you continuously strive to acquire new knowledge, skills and perspectives that will help you adapt to changes, improve your performance, and increase your chances of success.

One of the most insightful aspects of personal and professional development is identifying your strengths, and your areas for growth. This process of self-reflection can help you gain a deeper understanding of who you are, what you stand for, and what you are capable of. It involves taking a personal inventory of your skills, interests, values, and passions, and reflecting on your past experiences, both successes and failures. By doing so, you can identify the areas in which you excel, the ones you enjoy the most, and the ones where you may need to improve.

For example, if you're an entrepreneur, you may find that you have a great sense of creativity and a strong ability to spot opportunities. However, you may not have as much experience with financial planning and budgeting. Recognising these strengths and areas for growth can help you focus your development efforts and create a plan to build on your strengths and improve in areas where you're weaker. You could decide to take a course on financial management, or find a mentor who has experience in that field to guide you through the process.

Find a mentor who has more experience and can offer guidance, advice, and support as you navigate the challenges of starting and growing your business. They could provide you with valuable insights, share their experience and help you avoid common mistakes. A mentor might also be able to help you expand your network, open new doors, and expose you to new opportunities.

You can find a mentor in your industry or in a related field, and there are myriad different ways to connect with them, such as through professional associations, networking groups, or online platforms. Additionally, you can seek out support from family and friends, who can provide a sounding board for your ideas, offer valuable perspective on your business, and provide emotional support during the ups and downs of the journey.

Furthermore, it's also important to have self-awareness of not only your strengths and weaknesses but also your limitations, in terms of the time, resources, and capabilities that you have. It's important to set realistic goals and not to bite more than you can chew, otherwise, you could get overwhelmed and demotivated.

By identifying your strengths and areas for growth, and seeking out mentorship and support, you can take steps to improve your skills, increase your chances of success and work towards achieving your full potential. Remember that the journey is ongoing and adaptable, and it's essential to always be open to learning and growing.

TAKEAWAY TIPS:

1. The importance of continuous learning and development cannot be overstated. This includes staying up-to-date with industry trends and developments, taking courses or workshops to learn new skills, and always looking for opportunities to grow and improve.

2. Identifying your strengths and areas for growth is an important step in personal and professional development. This includes understanding your strengths and limitations, and focusing on areas where you can improve or learn new skills.

3. Seeking mentorship and support is an important part of personal and professional development. This can include seeking out a mentor who can offer guidance and advice or joining a professional association or community to connect with like-minded individuals.

CHAPTER 16:
BALANCING WORK AND PERSONAL LIFE

When you're working on turning your side hustle into a busy career, it's easy to get caught up in the excitement and dedication to your new project. However, it's important to remember that maintaining balance in your life is crucial for your well-being and success in the long run.

Balancing work and personal life is understanding the importance of work-life integration. This means that rather than trying to separate your work and personal life, you find ways to integrate them in a way that works for you. This can include setting boundaries, creating a schedule that allows for flexibility, and finding ways to make your work align with your personal values and goals.

There are several strategies that can help with managing work-life integration. One effective strategy is setting clear boundaries around your working hours. This can include setting specific times during the day when you will not respond to work-related emails or calls, as well as dedicating specific days or times for focusing on personal or family responsibilities. Additionally, you can use tools such as time-tracking software or apps to help you stay on top of your workload and manage your time more effectively.

It's also important to create a support system for yourself. Surrounding yourself with people who understand and support your goals can be a valuable source of emotional and practical support. Whether it's friends, family, or a professional support group, it's important to have people in your life who can understand and support you when you're going through the ups and downs of building a business like a side hustle.

Finally, it's also important to find a way to disconnect, unwind and re-energize yourself. It's easy to get caught up in the excitement and energy of your side hustle and let it take over your life, but it's important to take regular breaks, schedule regular vacations, and make time for hobbies and activities that you enjoy. This can help you to disconnect, recharge, and come back to your work feeling refreshed and energized.

In conclusion, balancing work and personal life is an essential aspect of turning your side hustle into a healthy career. By understanding the importance of work-life integration, setting boundaries, prioritising self-care and protecting your well-being and mental health, creating a support system and making time to unwind and disconnect, you can find a balance that works for you and increase your chances of long-term success.

TAKEAWAY TIPS:

1. Maintain balance between work and your other life responsibilities. This includes taking time for yourself, spending time with loved ones, and taking care of your physical and mental health.

2. Strategies for managing work-life integration include setting clear boundaries, creating a schedule that works for you, and learning to say no when necessary.

3. Protecting your well-being and mental health is crucial for maintaining the balance with a side hustle. This includes taking care of your physical health, practicing self-care, and seeking support when needed.

CHAPTER 17:
BUILDING A STRONG SUPPORT NETWORK

When you're working to turn your side hustle into a prosperous career, it's important to remember that you don't have to go it alone. Having a strong support network of friends, family, and like-minded individuals can make all the difference in your success and well-being.

Build a strong support network starting with friends and family. These are the people who know you best and who are most likely to support and encourage you on your journey. They can offer practical help, such as lending a hand with tasks related to your side hustle, or simply being a sounding board for your ideas and concerns. They can also offer emotional support, being a shoulder to cry on when things get tough, or a cheerleader when you need a boost of confidence.

Seek support and encouragement from others in your field. This could include networking with other entrepreneurs, joining professional associations or networking groups, or connecting with like-minded individuals online. These connections can provide valuable resources and inspiration, as well as opportunities for collaboration and learning. They can also help you stay motivated and inspired, as you see others working towards similar goals. From this you could build enduring and lifelong friendships, aside from the business benefits.

Being part of a community of like-minded individuals is also an important aspect. This could include a group of peers who share your passion and can offer support, feedback and accountability. This is easier than ever given the online communities that now exist for every kind of passion and interest. Having a community of people to connect with will provide motivation and support, as well as a sense of belonging and camaraderie. This can be done by joining meetups, forums, or groups on social media, or even starting your own group if none exist in your area.

It's also important to remember that seeking support and building a network is not a one-time thing. It is a continuous process, as you progress in your journey, your needs and those of your support network will evolve. It's important to stay in touch and maintain your connections, and to be open to new opportunities for collaboration and learning as they arise.

By tapping into the support and encouragement of friends, family, and like-minded individuals, you can gain valuable resources and inspiration, stay motivated and inspired, and have a sense of belonging and camaraderie. Remember that building a strong support network is a continuous process and it's essential to maintain your connections and be open to new opportunities as they arise.

TAKEAWAY TIPS:

1. The role of friends and family in a side hustle is crucial for providing support and encouragement. This includes having a supportive partner or spouse, having friends and family who understand and support your business, and being open and honest with them about your goals and challenges.

2. Seeking support and encouragement from others is an important step in building a strong support network. This includes reaching out to other entrepreneurs, joining a business or professional association, or seeking out a mentor or coach.

3. Building a community of like-minded individuals is an important step in building a strong support network. This could include joining a business or professional association, participating in networking events, or joining an online community of entrepreneurs.

CHAPTER 18:

OVERCOMING SELF-DOUBT AND IMPOSTER SYNDROME

When you're working to turn your side hustle into a flourishing career, it's natural to experience moments of self-doubt and imposter syndrome. These feelings can stem from a variety of challenges and pitfalls that are common when starting and growing a business, such as not feeling like you have enough experience or qualifications, feeling like a bit of a fraud due to your limited skills, or doubting your ability to succeed.

Imposter syndrome is a well-known psychological pattern in which an individual doubts their accomplishments and has a persistent fear of being exposed as a "fraud". This can be especially prevalent among entrepreneurs, who may feel that they don't have the same level of qualifications or experience as their peers, or that they don't truly belong in the business world. Imposter syndrome can also manifest in a sense of self-doubt, where individuals may question their ability to achieve their goals, or doubt the value of their ideas. Of course, these psychological doubts are valid, and they also fly in the face of the current trends to "fake it 'til you make it" that dominate social media.

The good news is that there are strategies for overcoming self-doubt and imposter syndrome. One effective strategy is to educate yourself about the feelings and symptoms of imposter syndrome, so you can recognize when it's affecting you, and then take steps to combat it. Another strategy is to reframe your thinking, by focusing on your strengths, accomplishments, and progress instead of dwelling on your weaknesses and failures. We've already highlighted just how important it is to seek out the support of others, whether it's friends and family, a therapist, or a support group for entrepreneurs, who can provide a sounding board, encouragement, and a sense of belonging.

Adopt a growth mindset to be open to learning, growth, and change. Instead of seeing mistakes as a failure, see them as opportunities to learn and improve. It's also important to take risks and push yourself out of your comfort zone. Taking risks can help you to build confidence, and it also helps to show you that you're capable of handling more than you think.

Having said that it's also important to have a realistic perspective on the process. Entrepreneurship is not a linear journey and there will be setbacks, challenges, and there will be failures. Recognize that these are all part of the process, and that failure is not a reflection of your personal worth but rather a learning opportunity.

Remind yourself that self-doubt and imposter syndrome are common challenges when turning a side hustle into a thriving career. However, by educating yourself about these feelings, seeking support, reframing your thinking, adopting a growth mindset, and having a realistic perspective, you can overcome these challenges and build confidence and resilience. Remember that it's a journey and that progress takes time. Be positive with yourself and celebrate the small wins along the way!

TAKEAWAY TIPS:

1. Common challenges and pitfalls in a side hustle include feeling overwhelmed, experiencing self-doubt or imposter syndrome, and facing rejection or failure.

2. Strategies for overcoming self-doubt and imposter syndrome include identifying and challenging negative thoughts, seeking support from others, and reminding yourself of your successes and accomplishments.

3. Building confidence and resilience is key in overcoming self-doubt and imposter syndrome. This includes setting realistic goals, celebrating small wins, and learning from setbacks and failures.

EXAMPLE:

Self-doubt and imposter syndrome were regularly plaguing Kyle, a freelance photographer. He often felt like he wasn't good enough or that his work wasn't worthy of being seen by others. He often compared himself to more successful photographers and felt like he would never be able to reach their level of success.

To overcome these challenges, Kyle began to implement a few strategies. He started to keep a gratitude journal and would write down at least three things he was grateful for every day. This helped him to focus on the positive aspects of his life and business, rather than dwelling on the negative. It built his self-confidence.

He also began to seek out feedback and constructive criticism from other photographers and industry professionals, which helped him to identify areas for improvement and to build a sense of community and support. Additionally, he began to focus on his strengths, and to celebrate his achievements, no matter how small, and this led to him being proud of everything he had started to achieve.

Kyle was able to overcome his self-doubt and imposter syndrome, and his business began to grow. He learned that building confidence and resilience is key to overcoming self-doubt and imposter syndrome, and that seeking support, feedback, and constructive criticism is crucial for growth and success. He also realized that gratitude and self-compassion are essential in the journey of building a successful side hustle.

"Don't let yesterday take
up too much of today."

– *Will Rogers*

CHAPTER 19:
MANAGING STRESS AND BURNOUT

When you're working to turn your side hustle into a effective career, it's important to be aware of the potential for stress and burnout. The demands of starting and growing a business can be significant, and if you're not careful, they could take a toll on your physical and mental health.

One of the key aspects of managing stress and burnout is the importance of self-care. Self-care includes taking care of your physical and mental well-being through regular exercise, healthy eating, and getting enough sleep. It also includes taking time for yourself, doing activities that you enjoy, and setting boundaries between your work and personal life. It's important to make self-care a priority, and to schedule regular time for it, in the same way that you would schedule any other important task.

Be aware of the signs of stress and burnout. Some of the common signs include feelings of exhaustion, irritability, and a lack of motivation. You may also experience physical symptoms such as headaches, muscle tension, and difficulty sleeping. If you're experiencing any of these symptoms, it's important to take action to manage your stress and prevent burnout.

There are several strategies for managing stress and maintaining a work-life balance. One effective strategy is to set boundaries and establish a schedule that allows for flexibility. This can include setting specific times during the day when you will not respond to work-related emails or calls, as well as dedicating specific days or times for focusing on personal or family responsibilities. Additionally, you can use tools such as time-tracking software or apps to help you stay on top of your workload and manage your time more effectively.

Another strategy is to prioritize self-care, and to make time for regular exercise, healthy eating, and other activities that promote well-being. Taking regular breaks, practicing mindfulness and meditation, and getting enough sleep are also essential for maintaining balance and staying focused and energized in your work.

It's also important to find a way to disconnect, unwind and re-energize yourself. It's easy to get caught up in the excitement of your side hustle and let it take over your life, but it's important to take regular breaks, schedule regular vacations, and make time for hobbies and activities that you enjoy. This can help you to disconnect, recharge, and come back to your work feeling refreshed and energized.

Managing stress and burnout is an essential aspect of turning your side hustle into a fruitful career. By prioritizing self-care, being aware of the signs of stress and burnout, and implementing strategies for managing stress and maintaining a work-life balance, you can prevent burnout and increase your chances of long-term success. Remember to be kind to yourself and take care of your well-being, it's the foundation of the journey.

TAKEAWAY TIPS:

1. The importance of self-care in a side hustle cannot be overstated. This includes taking care of your physical and mental health, setting boundaries, and making time for rest and relaxation.

2. Signs of stress and burnout include feeling constantly exhausted, lacking motivation, and experiencing physical or mental health symptoms.

3. Strategies for managing stress and maintaining work-life balance include setting realistic goals, prioritizing self-care, and learning to say no when necessary. It also includes developing a solid time management and organization skills, delegating tasks, and learning to set boundaries.

CHAPTER 20:
LEVERAGING YOUR SIDE HUSTLE FOR CAREER ADVANCEMENT

As you work to turn your side hustle into a successful business, it's important to remember that it can also serve as a valuable tool for career advancement. A well-chosen side hustle might provide valuable skills, experience, and connections that can help you take the next step in your main career.

One of the key benefits of a side hustle for career development is that it allows you to gain experience in a field or industry that you're interested in, without committing to a full-time job. This can include learning new skills, such as marketing, budgeting, or project management, which could be valuable for your career growth. A side hustle can also help you develop a strong network of contacts, which can be valuable for finding new opportunities and making connections.

Another benefit is that it allows you to take control of your career development, by identifying opportunities for growth and advancement. This can include identifying the skills and experience you need to take the next step in your career, and then taking steps to acquire those skills and gain that experience. This can include taking courses, attending workshops, or seeking out mentorship, all of which can help you build the skills and experience you need to advance in your career.

It's also important to be open and communicate your goals and aspirations with your main employer, or any potential new employer. You may choose to keep your side hustle to yourself, or you might consider demonstrating how your side hustle experience and skills will benefit the company. This could be done through creating a pitch deck to showcase any case studies, data or statistics that support your argument.

A side hustle can be a valuable tool for career advancement, by providing valuable skills, experience, and connections that can help you take the next step in your main career. By identifying opportunities for growth and advancement, making a clear business plan and communicating your aspirations and goals, building a strong network of contacts and being realistic about timing and planning, you can leverage your side hustle to advance in your career and achieve your professional goals.

TAKEAWAY TIPS:

1. The benefits of a side hustle for career development include gaining new skills, building a professional network, and developing a deeper understanding of your industry or field.

2. Identifying opportunities for growth and advancement is crucial for leveraging your side hustle for career advancement. This includes looking for opportunities to take on new responsibilities, gain new skills, or move up in your current company or field.

3. Making the transition from a side hustle to a full-time career is a big step, and it requires careful planning and preparation. This includes assessing the feasibility of your business, identifying any potential challenges or risks, and developing a plan for making the transition.

"The biggest risk is not taking any risk. In a world that's changing quickly, the only strategy that is guaranteed to fail is not taking risks."

– *Mark Zuckerberg*

CHAPTER 21:
SCALING YOUR SIDE HUSTLE

As your side hustle begins to gain momentum and show potential for growth, it's important to consider how to take it to the next level. Scaling your side hustle involves assessing its potential for growth, developing a plan for scaling, and managing the challenges of growth and expansion.

One of the first steps in scaling your side hustle is assessing its potential for growth. This includes evaluating its current revenue, customer base, and potential market size. It's important to identify your key customers and target markets, as well as identifying potential areas for expansion. This can include new product or service offerings, or entering new geographical markets.

Once you've assessed the potential for growth, the next step is to develop a plan for scaling your side hustle. This plan should include strategies for increasing revenue, expanding your customer base, and managing the challenges of growth and expansion. Some strategies that can help with scaling include investing in marketing and advertising, hiring additional staff or outsourcing certain tasks, and automating certain processes to streamline your business operations.

Identify and manage the potential challenges that come with scaling your business. One of the biggest challenges is the ability to handle increased demand for your product or service, which may require additional resources or personnel. You might also need to consider potential infrastructure requirements such as technology, logistics, and inventory management.

As you scale your side hustle, it's important to maintain strong financial management and control. As we talked about earlier in the book, this includes creating and sticking to a budget, forecasting and planning, and monitoring performance and metrics to measure the success of your scaling efforts. This is why those early number-crunching sessions matter!

Remember that as your business grows, it's important to keep a close eye on your finances, monitor performance, and be prepared to adapt your strategy as needed. Assessing growth from year to year, increases in costs, percentages of profit for particular services or goods, and all the metrics that your records can provide is going to be vital.

Another challenge that comes with scaling is managing the risk and uncertainty. It's important to have a solid understanding of the risks involved and have a plan in place to mitigate and manage them. This could include diversifying revenue streams, implementing contingencies plans and insurance.

Scaling your side hustle is a vital step if you are to take the step to turn it into a productive career. By assessing its potential for growth, developing a plan for scaling, and managing the challenges of growth and expansion, you can take your side hustle to the next level and increase your chances of success.

TAKEAWAY TIPS:

1. Assessing the potential for growth is an important step in scaling your side hustle. This includes evaluating the size of your market, understanding your target audience, and identifying opportunities for expansion.

2. Developing a plan for scaling your side hustle is crucial for achieving success. This includes identifying the resources you need, setting clear goals, and developing a strategy for growth.

3. Managing the challenges of growth and expansion is an important part of scaling your side hustle. This includes dealing with increased competition, managing cash flow, and finding the right talent to help you grow.

CHAPTER 22:
DIVERSIFYING YOUR INCOME STREAMS

As a dedicated side hustler, diversifying your income streams is an important step in turning your passion into a flourishing career. Diversifying your income refers to having multiple sources of income, rather than relying on just one. This can provide a safety net in case one income stream dries up suddenly, and it can also help you to grow your income and achieve financial stability.

One of the key benefits of diversifying your income streams is that it can provide a safety net in case one income stream starts to slow down. For example, if you're a freelancer, and you lose one major client, having multiple streams of income can help cushion the blow and provide a sense of financial security. Additionally, having multiple streams of income will also help you grow your income over time, and achieve financial stability.

Diversifying your income streams can help you to be more resilient to market changes and trends, which can be especially important for side hustlers who may be operating in highly competitive markets or dealing with unpredictable income.

The first step in diversifying your income streams is to identify additional opportunities for income. This could include offering additional products or services, or you could consider branching out into affiliate marketing or sponsored content, or creating digital products like ebooks, courses, and webinars.

Have a plan to balance multiple sources of income. This can include setting clear goals and tracking your progress, managing your time effectively, and being organized and efficient with your efforts. It's also important to establish clear budgets for each income stream and distinct financial plans, and to be mindful of the potential risks associated with multiple income streams.

It's also important to note that diversifying your income streams is not a one-time task, it's a continuous process. As your business grows, it's important to regularly re-evaluate your income streams, and to be open to new opportunities as they arise.

Remember that diversifying your income streams is a continuous process and it's essential to be open to new opportunities as they arise. By identifying additional income streams and opportunities, and by having a plan to balance multiple sources of income, you can achieve financial stability and be more resilient to market changes and trends.

TAKEAWAY TIPS:

1. As soon as your side hustle allows it, work towards diversifying your income streams, so that you are not reliant on a single source of income.

2. Continually identifying additional income streams and opportunities is an important step in diversifying your income. Constantly be on the look-out for new business

opportunities, work to develop new products or services, and find creative ways to monetize your existing assets.

3. Balancing multiple sources of income is an important part of diversifying your income. This includes setting clear goals and priorities, managing your time and resources, and developing a plan to make sure your income streams are working together effectively.

EXAMPLE:

Angela, with a side hustle as a freelance writer, relied heavily on writing projects once she was made redundant from her day job. She realized that this was not a sustainable way to earn a living and that she needed to find additional income streams.

To overcome this challenge, Angela began to explore new opportunities. She started to take on writing projects for other publications, and began to teach writing workshops and classes. She also started to write and publish her own e-book which helped her to earn additional income. Additionally, she started to explore affiliate marketing and sponsored posts on her blog to earn passive income.

Angela was able to quickly diversify her income and create multiple streams of income. She learned that diversifying her income is crucial for her financial stability and security. She also realized that it's important to be open to new opportunities and to continuously explore new ways to earn money.

She also learned the importance of balancing her time and efforts between her multiple income streams to make sure that none of them was neglected.

CHAPTER 23:
BUILDING A STRONG PERSONAL BRAND

When turning your side hustle into a prosperous career, building a strong personal brand is an essential step. Personal branding is the process of creating a unique image, message and reputation that represents you and your business. A strong personal brand can help you to stand out in a crowded marketplace, and to attract the right customers and opportunities.

One of the key aspects of building a strong personal brand is identifying your unique value proposition. Your unique value proposition is the unique benefit that you offer to your customers. This could include your skills, experience, or the unique approach you take to your business. By identifying and communicating your unique value proposition, you'll be able to differentiate yourself from your competitors and attract the right customers.

Another important aspect is creating consistent messaging across all of your platforms. This includes creating a consistent tone, style, and message across your website, social media, and any other marketing materials you use. This will help to create a cohesive image and message that represents you and your business, and that resonates with your target audience.

Build a strong personal brand online and offline. This includes creating a professional website, social media presence and building a strong network offline. This consistency creates credibility, and it's essential to attracting the right customers and opportunities as your business scales.

Building a personal brand also involves being intentional and consistent with your actions and communication, being authentic and transparent, and keeping an open mind to feedback and improvement. In addition, by consistently delivering high-quality services or products, you are also building a reputation, and reputation can be a powerful asset when it comes to building a personal brand.

By identifying your unique value proposition and messaging, creating consistency across all platforms and building a strong personal brand online and offline, you'll be able to stand out in a crowded marketplace, attract the right customers and opportunities, and increase your chances of success. Remember that building a personal brand takes time, consistency and continuous effort.

TAKEAWAY TIPS:

1. The role of personal branding in a side hustle is important because it helps you stand out and differentiate yourself from your competition.

2. Identifying your unique value proposition and messaging is an important step in building a strong personal brand. This includes understanding your strengths and what makes you unique, and communicating this effectively to your target audience.

3. Building a strong personal brand online and offline is an important step in building a successful side hustle. This includes creating a strong online presence, building a professional network, and leveraging your personal brand to create opportunities for growth and advancement.

CHAPTER 24:
COLLABORATING AND LEVERAGING PARTNERSHIPS

Collaborating and leveraging partnerships can be a valuable strategy for turning your side hustle into a career. Partnerships and collaborations can provide a range of benefits, including access to new customers, resources, and expertise.

One of the key benefits of collaborating and partnering in a side hustle is that it can help you to access new customers and markets. By partnering with other businesses or organizations, you can tap into their customer base and reach new audiences. Additionally, partnerships can also provide access to new resources, such as equipment, technology, or expertise, that can help you to grow your business.

You'll find that another benefit of partnerships and collaborations is that they can help you to gain credibility and build your reputation. When you collaborate with established businesses or organizations, you can leverage their reputation and credibility to help promote your own business.

The first step in collaborating and leveraging partnerships is to identify potential partners and to evaluate the potential value of the partnership. This can include considering factors such as the size and reach of the potential partner, their reputation and credibility, and the potential for mutual benefit.

Once you've identified potential partners, the next step is to approach them to negotiate the terms of the partnership. This can include discussing the scope of the partnership, the roles and responsibilities of each party, and the financial and legal aspects of the partnership.

To maximize the value of partnerships and collaborations, it's important to establish clear goals and objectives, and to communicate and collaborate effectively. It's also important to regularly evaluate and re-evaluate the partnership, and to be open to discussing any issues or concerns that may arise.

Additionally, it's important to have a plan in place for managing and resolving any conflicts that may arise, it's important to keep in mind that not every partnership will be a success and be prepared to handle any potential challenges. You may need legal advice on the specifics, or you might decide to keep things informal, but be aware that even a simple written agreement might help iron out difficulties later.

In identifying potential partners, negotiating the terms of the partnership, and effectively communicating and collaborating, you can access new customers, resources and expertise, gain credibility, and build your reputation. Remember to be open-minded, flexible and be prepared to handle any challenges that may arise.

TAKEAWAY TIPS:

1. The benefits of collaborating and partnering in a side hustle include gaining access to new resources, building a professional network, and expanding your reach and impact.

2. Identifying potential partners and negotiating terms is an important step in developing successful partnerships. This includes assessing the compatibility of your goals and values, and understanding the strengths and limitations of potential partners.

3. Maximizing the value of partnerships and collaborations is crucial for achieving success in a side hustle. This includes setting clear goals, developing effective communication and decision-making processes, and building trust and open communication with your partners.

"I have not failed. I've just found 10,000 ways that won't work."

– Thomas Edison

CHAPTER 25:
OVERCOMING CHALLENGES AND SETBACKS

As a side hustler, it's important to be prepared for challenges and setbacks, as they are a natural part of any entrepreneurial journey. While these challenges can be difficult to overcome, they can also provide valuable learning opportunities and help you to grow as an entrepreneur.

Common challenges and setbacks faced by side hustlers include difficulty in finding customers, lack of funding, and balancing the demands of a side hustle with a full-time job. Additionally, side hustlers may also face challenges such as competition, market changes, and setbacks such as financial losses or product failures.

Have a developed plan in place for handling these challenges. This could include having a clear strategy for acquiring customers, identifying potential future sources of funding, and planning out your time effectively. By now, you know how important it is to be adaptable and open to new opportunities as they arise, and to be prepared to pivot your strategy as needed.

Maintain momentum by setting small, achievable goals, and by taking consistent, incremental steps towards your long-term goals.

This can help to keep you motivated and focused on your goals, even when faced with setbacks or challenges.

When faced with a setback, it's also important to take a step back and reflect on what went wrong, and to learn from your mistakes. This can help you to identify areas for improvement and to come up with a new plan for moving forward. Additionally, seeking advice from the experienced entrepreneurs you have met along the way, or business mentors, can be a valuable tool for learning from failures and setbacks.

Don't forget, overcoming challenges and setbacks is a natural part of the entrepreneurial journey. By having a plan in place, maintaining momentum and being adaptable, and by learning from failures and setbacks, you can continue to move forward and achieve your goals as a side hustler. Remember that every setback or failure is an opportunity to learn, grow and improve your strategy.

TAKEAWAY TIPS:

1. Common challenges and setbacks faced by side hustlers include lack of time, lack of funding, and difficulty finding customers.

2. Strategies for overcoming challenges and maintaining momentum include setting realistic goals, breaking down big tasks into smaller steps, and seeking support from others.

3. Learning from failures and setbacks is an important part of achieving success in a side hustle. This includes analysing what went wrong, identifying areas for improvement, and creating a plan to prevent similar issues in the future.

EXAMPLE:

One of the most common challenges faced by side hustlers is a lack of time. As a busy working mother of two young children, Ashley struggled to find the time to work on her side hustle, a handmade jewellery business. She found herself constantly putting her business on the back burner, and her sales and growth were stagnant.

To overcome this challenge, Ashley implemented a few strategies. She began setting realistic goals and breaking down tasks into smaller, manageable steps. She also started making better use of her time by using tools like a planner and scheduling software to stay organized and prioritize her tasks. Additionally, she sought support from her family and friends, by asking for help with her children for a few weeks, which helped her to have some dedicated time for her business.

Ashley was able to overcome her time constraints and see significant growth in her business. She learned that by setting realistic goals, breaking down tasks, and seeking support, she was able to maintain momentum and overcome the challenge of time constraints. She realised that the most important thing she could do is to stay positive and persevere through the tough times, and use them as an opportunity to grow and learn.

CHAPTER 26:
STAYING UP-TO-DATE AND RELEVANT

Staying up-to-date and relevant is crucial for any side hustler looking to turn their passion into an effective career. As the market and industry changes, it's important to stay current and adapt to these changes to remain competitive and succeed in your field.

Understand the changes happening in your industry, and always be alive to identifying new trends and opportunities. For example, staying current on new technologies or changes in consumer preferences can help you to identify new opportunities for growth and to stay ahead of the competition. Staying up-to-date can also help you to identify potential challenges and risks, and to take proactive steps to mitigate them.

To stay up-to-date, it's important to identify sources of industry news and updates. This can include subscribing to industry publications, attending relevant conferences, following thought leaders and influencers in your field, and engaging in online communities related to your industry. Additionally, staying active in professional organizations, attending workshops, and attending seminars and webinars on topics related to your business can also be a great way to stay updated.

Another important aspect of staying up-to-date and relevant is to continuously learn and adapt to changes in your field. This can include staying informed on best practices, experimenting with new strategies, and being open to feedback and new ideas. Additionally, being open to learning new skills, such as new software or technologies, can help you to stay competitive and to adapt to changes in your industry.

Staying relevant is crucial for any side hustler looking to turn their passion into a thriving career. By identifying sources of industry news and updates, continuously learning, adapting to changes in your field, and taking steps to stay current and relevant, you can increase your chances of success and remain competitive. Remember that staying up-to-date and relevant is a continuous process – make time for it in your schedule!

TAKEAWAY TIPS:

1. Stay up-to-date with industry trends, developments, and best practices.

2. Identifying reliable sources of industry news and updates is an important step in staying current and relevant. This includes subscribing to industry publications, following thought leaders in your field, and participating in online communities.

3. Continuously learning and adapting to changes in your field is crucial for staying current and relevant. This includes taking courses or workshops, reading industry publications, and staying open to new ideas and perspectives.

CHAPTER 27:

LEVERAGING YOUR SIDE HUSTLE FOR NETWORKING AND PROFESSIONAL DEVELOPMENT

Networking and professional development are essential components of turning your side hustle into a burgeoning career. Not only do they help you to build relationships and gain visibility in your industry, but they also provide opportunities for personal and professional growth.

One of the key benefits of networking and professional development for a side hustle is the ability to connect with other entrepreneurs and industry professionals. Building relationships with other business owners, leaders and experts in your field can help you to gain valuable insights, knowledge and support. Additionally, networking can also provide access to potential customers, investors, and partners, which can help you to grow your business.

Another benefit of networking and professional development is the opportunity for personal and professional growth. By participating in workshops, conferences, and other events, you can gain new knowledge, skills, and perspectives that can help you to improve your business and your professional development.

The first step in leveraging your side hustle for networking and professional development is to identify opportunities for networking and personal growth. This could include attending industry conferences, joining professional organizations, or attending networking events in your local area. Additionally, considering taking on a mentor – or even a mentee – as this can be a great way to gain insight and knowledge from more experienced professionals.

Make the most of these opportunities. When attending networking events or conferences, it's important to come prepared with business cards, an elevator pitch, and a clear idea of the people you would like to connect with. Additionally, when seeking mentorship, it's important to have clear goals and objectives and to make the most of your time with the mentor by being well prepared.

By identifying opportunities for networking and personal growth, and making the most of them, you can build relationships, gain visibility and knowledge, and improve your personal and professional development. Remember to be strategic and intentional in your approach, and to actively seek out opportunities for growth.

TAKEAWAY TIPS:

1. The benefits of networking and professional development for a side hustle include gaining new contacts, learning new skills, and building a professional network.

2. Identifying opportunities for networking and personal growth is an important step in leveraging your side hustle for networking and professional development. This includes joining professional associations, attending conferences

and workshops, and seeking out mentorship and coaching opportunities.

3. Making the most of conferences, workshops, and other events is an important step in leveraging your side hustle for networking and professional development. This includes a plan for the sort of connections you would like to make, preparing well ahead of time, networking with other attendees, and following up with new contacts after the event.

CHAPTER 28:
THE FUTURE OF SIDE HUSTLES AND ENTREPRENEURSHIP

The world of side hustles and entrepreneurship is constantly evolving, and it's important for side hustlers to stay informed about the latest trends and developments to prepare for the future. Whether you're just starting out or have been running your side hustle for years, understanding the future of side hustles and entrepreneurship can help you to stay competitive and to capitalize on new opportunities.

One of the key trends in the world of side hustles and entrepreneurship is the rise of the gig economy. The gig economy refers to the growing number of people who are working as independent contractors or freelancers, rather than as traditional employees. This trend is driven by factors such as the availability of technology and platforms that make it easier to connect with clients and customers, and a desire for more flexibility and autonomy in work. There are well-publicised downsides to this economic model that are likely subject to future revision, but you may find that for your side hustle, the gig economy offers you flexible access to many external professionals for short assignments, whether for example for design work or legal advice, that give mutual benefits.

Notably, another important trend is the increasing importance of technology in entrepreneurship. The rise of automation, machine learning, and artificial intelligence is changing the way businesses operate and is creating new opportunities for entrepreneurs. For example, technology-enabled platforms such as e-commerce marketplaces and affiliate marketing platforms are making it easier for side hustlers to connect with customers, and the growth of automated processes is creating opportunities for entrepreneurs to enter industries that have traditionally been closed to small businesses.

Finally, in the current era, we have seen that remote work and an online presence has become increasingly important due to the impact of the COVID-19 pandemic. Remote work has been a trend that is expected to continue, and many businesses are adapting to digital channels to reach their customers, thus making a strong online presence even more important.

To prepare for the future of side hustles and entrepreneurship, it's important to stay informed about the latest trends and developments and to be adaptable and willing to change. This could include learning new skills, such as coding or digital marketing, and embracing new technologies and platforms. It's important to have a plan in place for dealing with changes in your industry or market, and to be open to new opportunities as they arise.

The world of side hustles and entrepreneurship is constantly evolving, and it's important to stay informed about the latest trends and developments. By understanding the future of commerce, staying adaptable, and preparing for the future, you can stay competitive and capitalize on new opportunities.

Remember to stay curious and be open to learning new things to stay ahead of the game!

TAKEAWAY TIPS:

1. Trends and developments in the world of side hustles and entrepreneurship include the growth of the gig economy, the increasing popularity of online platforms and marketplaces, and the rise of remote work and digital nomads.

2. The potential for future growth and opportunities in side hustles includes the continued growth of the gig economy, the increasing demand for online and e-commerce businesses, and the emergence of new technologies and platforms.

3. Preparing for the future of work and entrepreneurship includes staying informed about trends and developments, developing new skills and knowledge, and being open to new opportunities.

"The only limit to our realization of tomorrow will be our doubts of today."

- Franklin D. Roosevelt

CHAPTER 29:
CONCLUSION: TURNING YOUR PASSION INTO A THRIVING CAREER

As you come to the end of this book, I hope you have a better understanding of the process of turning your passion into a successful career. Starting a side hustle can be – at the same time – a challenging and rewarding journey. However, I firmly believe that with the right approach, and a strategy that is flexible, it's possible to turn your passion into a successful and fulfilling career.

Throughout this book, I have discussed a wide range of topics and provided actionable advice to help you to turn your passion into a triumphant career. From identifying your niche and developing a business plan, to marketing your business and building a strong online presence, I have covered the key steps you need to take to turn your passion into a successful side hustle.

One of the key takeaways from this book is the importance from the outset of identifying your niche, your target market and understanding your customer's needs. By focusing on a specific niche and tailoring your products or services to meet the needs of your target market, you can increase your chances of success. Additionally, developing a well-structured and actionable business plan is crucial for any side hustle. It will help you to set clear goals, map out your strategy and stay on track.

Another important takeaway is the importance of building a strong online presence. In today's digital age, having a professional-looking website and an active presence on social media can help you to reach a wider audience, establish credibility, and grow your business. Additionally, networking and professional development are also key to success. Building relationships, gaining visibility and knowledge, and improving your personal and professional development will increase your chances of success.

Finally, always remember that starting a side hustle should not just be about making money, but also about exploring your passions and achieving a sense of fulfilment. By turning your hobby or interest into a thriving career, you could enjoy the freedom and autonomy that comes with being your own boss, and you can find satisfaction and purpose in the work that you do.

With the right approach and dedication, all of this and more is achievable. This book has provided you with key insights, actionable advice, and practical tips to help you turn your passion into a successful and fulfilling side hustle. Remember to stay focused on your goals, be willing to take risks and to learn from your failures. Keep in mind that building a business takes time, it will take effort and it will certainly take dedication. Stay true to your passion and be persistent, and the rewards of turning your passion into a career can be truly fulfilling.

I wish you luck on your journey!

TAKEAWAY TIPS:

1. Understand the value to other people of your passion, and carefully research find ways to turn it into a business.

2. Key takeaways and lessons learned from the book include the importance of setting realistic goals, seeking support and guidance, and staying focused on your passions and purpose.

3. With effort and dedication, the potential for success and fulfilment through a side hustle can be substantial. Build the right mindset, strategies, and support, and remind yourself that turning your passion into a thriving career is within reach.

4. It's important to remember that starting a side hustle is a process and it's important to be flexible and adaptable, to learn from mistakes and to persevere in the face of challenges.

CASE STUDIES

CASE STUDY 1: FROM BLOGGER TO BUSINESS OWNER: THE STORY OF MIA'S SIDE HUSTLE

Mia had always been passionate about cooking and food, and had been blogging about her recipes and cooking experiences for several years. She had built up a loyal following of readers who enjoyed her unique perspective on food and cooking. However, as a full-time employee, she never considered turning her hobby into a business.

One day, while discussing her blog with a co-worker, Mia realized that she had an opportunity to turn her passion into a side hustle. She decided to take the leap and start her own small business creating and selling her own homemade marinades and sauces.

Mia validated her business idea by conducting market research and surveying her blog readers. She discovered that there was a demand for her homemade marinades and sauces and that her readers would be interested in buying them.

Using her minimal budget, Mia started small, selling her products at local farmers' markets, and through her blog's online store. Through her website, she was able to reach her targeted market, building her customer base and establishing her brand.

As her business grew, she started to leverage her personal branding and online presence, by developing and optimising her website and social media accounts, following the advice from "Building a Strong Online Presence" and "Building a Strong Personal Brand".

Mia's side hustle continued to grow, and she eventually quit her full-time job to focus on her business. She was able to scale her business by diversifying her income streams, as advised in "Diversifying Your Income Streams" and "Scaling Your Side Hustle".

Today, Mia's marinades and sauces are sold in several local grocery stores and her business continues to expand. She is grateful for the opportunity to turn her passion into a flourishing career and is proud to be able to share her love for food with others.

This case study illustrates how, with the right approach and dedication, it's possible to turn a passion into a successful and fulfilling side hustle. As Mia shows, a side hustle can provide the flexibility and autonomy that comes with being your own boss, and can lead to a sense of satisfaction and purpose. By following the key steps outlined in the book, "From Side Hustle to Success: Turning Your Passion into a Thriving Career", anyone can turn their passion into a profitable and successful side hustle.

CASE STUDY: FROM HANDMADE TO HIGH-DEMAND: THE STORY OF MICHAEL'S SIDE HUSTLE

Michael had always been interested in woodworking and had been building wooden furniture and decor as a hobby for years. He had a small workshop in his garage and enjoyed creating unique and one-of-a-kind pieces. However, it was just a hobby and he never considered turning it into a business.

One day, at a community fair, Michael set up a small booth to display some of his handmade wooden creations. To his surprise, he sold out of all his products in just a few hours and received numerous requests for custom orders. He realized that there was a demand for his handmade wooden creations and decided to turn his hobby into a side hustle.

Michael started small, and he began by selling his wooden creations through online marketplaces and social media. He also began taking custom orders, which allowed him to make use of his niche knowledge and leverage his ability to create unique pieces.

As his business grew, Michael began to think about scaling his business and expanding his product line, following the advice contained in this book's chapters "Scaling Your Side Hustle" and

"Diversifying Your Income Streams". He began to experiment with different woods and techniques to create a wider variety of products.

Thanks to his online presence, Michael was able to reach a larger audience and increase his customer base, using the advice contained in this book. He also focused on personal and professional development, by taking workshops and attending trade shows, as advised in the chapter "Personal and Professional Development".

Today, Michael's business has grown into a successful and profitable side hustle, and he continues to create beautiful, handmade wooden products that are in high demand. He is proud to have turned his passion into a fruitful career, and is grateful for the opportunity to share his love of woodworking with others.

This case study illustrates how Michael was able to turn his hobby and passion into a successful and profitable side hustle by following the key steps outlined in this book, "From Side Hustle to Success: Turning Your Passion into a Thriving Career". Through experimentation and adaptation, he was able to create a successful business and create a unique and profitable niche for himself. It highlights the importance of being adaptable and open to change, as well as leveraging your strengths and knowledge to turn a hobby into a successful business. It also shows the importance of having a strong online presence, and of focusing on personal and professional development to reach your goals and be successful.

CASE STUDY: FROM SETBACK TO SUCCESS: THE STORY OF JESSICA'S SIDE HUSTLE

Jessica had always been passionate about photography and had been building her portfolio and skills for several years. She started her side hustle as a freelance photographer, shooting events and portraits, and quickly gained a reputation for her unique and creative style.

However, midway through her journey, Jessica faced a major setback when her camera equipment was stolen. This not only resulted in a financial loss but also emotional blow. Despite this setback, Jessica didn't give up. She saw this as an opportunity to take her photography in a new direction and decided to focus on mobile photography and videography.

With the strategies outlined in this book's chapter "Overcoming Challenges and Setbacks", Jessica was able to refocus her efforts, and began to experiment with mobile photography and videography. She leveraged the advice of the chapters "Building a Strong Online Presence" and "Building a Strong Personal Brand" to promote her work and attract clients.

To her surprise, Jessica found that mobile photography and videography suited her style and allowed her to be more creative and spontaneous. By focusing on mobile photography and videography, she was able to differentiate herself from the competition, and her business began to grow.

As she gained more clients, Jessica continued to build her brand and online presence, using the advice in the chapter "Personal and Professional Development" to improve her skills and knowledge and develop a unique style. She also started to collaborate with other photographers and videographers, leveraging the advice from "Collaborating and Leveraging Partnerships".

Today, Jessica's business is growing consistently, and her mobile photography and videography have become her major strength. She has developed a strong reputation for her unique and creative style and has built a loyal client base. Despite the setback she faced, she managed to turn it into a major strength, and she is proud to have turned her passion into a successful and fulfilling side hustle.

This case study illustrates how Jessica, despite facing a major problem, was able to turn it into an opportunity and find success by being open to change and experimenting with new techniques and technologies. It highlights the importance of building a strong online presence and personal brand, as well as continuously learning and developing one's skills and knowledge.

By leveraging the advice outlined in this book, "From Side Hustle to Success: Turning Your Passion into a Thriving Career", she was able to adapt to the challenges and setbacks and turn them into strengths. It serves as an inspiration and encouragement to us all that, even when things don't go as planned, there are always opportunities for growth and success.

FURTHER READING

1. "The Lean Startup" by Eric Ries: A step-by-step guide to starting a business, with a focus on using a "lean" methodology to test and validate business ideas.
2. "The $100 Startup" by Chris Guillebeau: A practical guide to starting a business with a minimal budget and focuses on finding and leveraging untapped resources.
3. "The E-Myth Revisited" by Michael E. Gerber: A classic on small business management, which explores the common misconceptions about starting a business and the importance of systematizing and delegating tasks for success.
4. "The Power of Your Leadership: Making a Difference with Others" by John C. Maxwell: This book explores the importance of leadership skills in business and provides practical advice for developing and honing leadership abilities.
5. "The Art of SEO" by Eric Enge, Stephan Spencer, and Jessie C. Stricchiola: A comprehensive guide to search engine optimization (SEO) and provides actionable advice for improving your website's visibility on search engines.
6. "The Art of Possibility" by Rosamund Stone Zander and Benjamin Zander: A fresh perspective on leadership and

innovation, encouraging the reader to embrace uncertainty and new possibilities.

7. "Business Model Generation" by Alexander Osterwalder and Yves Pigneur: A visual framework for designing and testing business models and a valuable resource for entrepreneurs and side hustlers looking to create a sustainable business.

8. "The 4-Hour Work Week" by Timothy Ferriss: A comprehensive guide to escaping the 9-to-5 grind and achieving financial freedom through lifestyle design and outsourcing.

9. "Crush It!: Why Now Is the Time to Cash in on Your Passion" by Gary Vaynerchuk: A motivational guide for entrepreneurs, and provides practical advice for turning your passion into a business and building a personal brand online.

www.ingramcontent.com/pod-product-compliance
Lightning Source LLC
Chambersburg PA
CBHW070552220526
45467CB00003B/1181